# GREAT BIBLE STORIES

# JONAH

## Adapted by Maxine Nodel    Illustrated by Norman Nodel

BARONET BOOKS is a registered trademark of Playmore Inc., Publishers
and Waldman Publishing Corp., New York, N.Y.

Copyright © MCMXCIII Playmore Inc., Publishers
and Waldman Publishing Corp., New York, New York

BARONET BOOKS, NEW YORK, NEW YORK
Printed in China

Once there was a Hebrew prophet named Jonah. One day God spoke to him, saying, "Go to the city of Nineveh and tell the people there to repent of their evil ways."

Nineveh was the capital of Assyria and the Assyrian empire was an enemy of Jonah's people. Jonah did not want to help them, so he ignored God's commands.

"Why should I go to Nineveh?" thought Jonah. "If I give those people God's message, perhaps they will change their ways. The city will never be destroyed."

Instead Jonah went to the seaport of Joppa where he boarded a ship going in the opposite direction.

Shortly after the ship set sail, a fierce hurricane blew across the windy sea. The captain and sailors were frightened and tossed cargo overboard to lighten the ship.

The sailors began to pray, each to his own god, as the captain went down into the ship. There, he found Jonah soundly asleep.

"Get up, Jonah!" he yelled. "A great storm is here!
Pray to your own god like everyone else!"

Jonah began to worry, because he thought God had sent the great hurricane. He told the crew how he had fled from God's commands.

"Are you to blame for the storm?" they asked.

"I am a Hebrew," replied Jonah. "I worship the God who made the seas and the land. This storm is my fault. You should throw me overboard."

The sailors grew scared and did not listen to Jonah.
They tried instead to navigate the ship toward safe harbor.

The waves grew higher and higher. The crew realized they were too far from land. They began praying again. "Lord, please don't let us lose our lives because of a single man."

Now they knew they had to get rid of Jonah. They picked him up and threw him overboard.

The storm vanished, as Jonah drifted away. Then he started to sink beneath the calm sea. Jonah felt his life was coming to an end.

Suddenly a great whale swam up to Jonah and swallowed him whole. Jonah stayed inside the great whale for three long days and three long nights!

Jonah sat in the belly of the whale and thought. "I was stupid to have fled from God's presence." But Jonah was lucky. God kept him safe.

Soon, God ordered the whale to put Jonah on land. God spoke again to Jonah, "Go to Nineveh and proclaim my message to all!"

This time Jonah obeyed.

The city of Nineveh was so big it took Jonah three full days to walk through it. After the first day, he thought it was time to give the people God's commands.

"Nineveh will be destroyed in forty days!" Jonah's message scared the people, for they knew they had been wicked. The people began to repent and change their ways.

The king heard Jonah's words and exclaimed, "No one in Nineveh shall eat or drink anything! They shall be covered in sackcloth and pray to the one God." So the people tried to rid their city of evil.

God saw that the people of Nineveh had repented. He was ready to forgive them and save their city. But Jonah was not happy with God's mercy.

Jonah called to God, "I knew you were a loving and merciful God, ready to forgive those who are truly sorry. So let me die, for now that I saved the enemy of my people, I am better off dead."

God tried to teach Jonah a lesson, for Jonah had not thought it right for the God of Israel to be merciful to the people of Nineveh.

Jonah had left the city and made himself a small shelter just outside the gates. It was very hot, so God made a tall leafy gourd for shade where Jonah sat.

The next morning a worm attacked the gourd. And at God's command, the gourd withered and died.

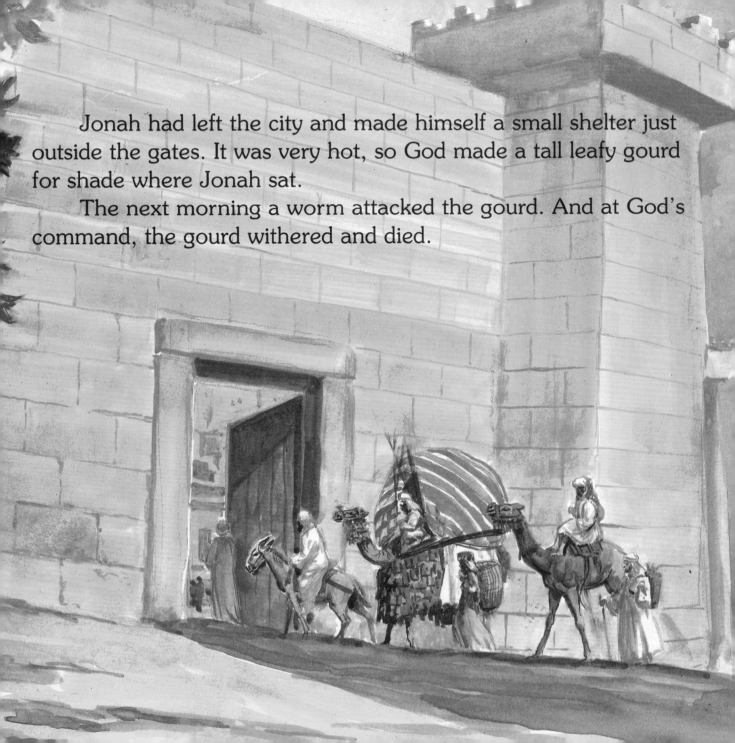

Jonah felt very sad and angry that the gourd had died. "Why do you feel sad for the gourd?" asked God.

God said, "This gourd grew up in the night, and disappeared the next day. Why do you pity it. You did nothing to make it grow!"

Jonah finally understood God's words. He realized that it was God who had made all the people of Nineveh, and that we must not oppose God's ways and wisdom.